Alaska Pioneer Interiors

A Child's Room. Valdez, Alaska, around 1910.
University of Alaska Archives, Mary Whalen Collection.
Photographer: P. S. Hunt.

Toys include a wooden Schoenhut circus on the first of the three bracketed shelves, early German stuffed animals, possibly Steiff, a Maggie and Jinx pair on the high shelf, a hobby horse on wheels, and a model windmill on the dresser.

Alaska Pioneer Interiors

An Annotated Photographic File

Jane G. Haigh

Alaska Historical Commission
Studies in History
No. 137

Tanana-Yukon Historical Society
Fairbanks, Alaska

Printed in the United States of America

LCC No. 86-51276

ISBN No. 0-940457-20-2

Publication of this project was supported by a grant from the State of Alaska, Alaska
Historical Commission, however, the author is responsible for all statements herein,
whether of fact or opinion.

Designed and Produced by Jane G. Haigh
Printed by Dragon Press, Delta Junction, Alaska

Published by the Tanana-Yukon Historical Society
P.O. Box 1336
Fairbanks, Alaska 99701

The Tanana-Yukon Historical Society is a non-profit organization

*Cover Photo: Wedding Gifts, Valdez, Alaska. November, 1909 by P.S. Hunt. University of
Alaska Archives, Mary Whalen Collection, see pages 52-53*

Contents

Preface

This book began as a project of the Tanana-Yukon Historical Society to furnish the historic Wickersham House at Alaskaland in Fairbanks, Alaska. Although Wickersham kept a detailed diary, there were no known photographs of the interior of the house. This led to a search for photographs of the interiors of other Alaskan houses of the period and a study of the Decorative Arts of the period in an effort to understand the material collected.

Rene Blahuta deserves credit for steering me to the P. S. Hunt photographs in the Mary Whalen Collection at the University of Alaska Archives. Without Jane Williams, however, there might have been no project. Jane has provided unfailing support and encouragement since the project got started in 1979.

The over one hundred photographs that were collected by the Historical Society and the research notes we used to develop a furnishing plan for the Wickersham House stayed filed away until 1984 when, through the generous assistance of The Alaska Historical Commission, I obtained a grant to complete the research and the manuscript. I would especially like to thank Jo Antonson and Bill Hanable of the Alaska Historical Commission.

For inspiration, I would like to thank William Seale whose excellent book *Tasteful Interlude* charted the path through the interpretation of photographs of historic interiors.

I would also like to thank Susan Pickle-Hedrick for helping to identify some of the objects and the many other people around town who encouraged me to publish this book.

Jane Galblum Haigh
Fairbanks, Alaska
July 1986

Introduction

A close look at these photographs, like peeking through the windows of an old house, provides a fascinating look at home life in some of Alaska's pioneer towns. In addition however, comparing and analyzing furnishings, furniture styles and arrangements, and such diverse elements as wallpaper, lamps, rugs, and other material objects can provide valuable information about people and lifestyles on the Alaskan frontier. One of the most common images is of an ornate Victorian parlour with flocked wallpaper and flounced and feathered everything. Another common and contrasting image is of board tables, moosehorn chairs and fur rugs. Rather than attempt to draw a single conclusion about an Alaskan pioneer style, I have attempted to present a wide range of elements that over a period of time comprised the pioneer home. Following a synopsis of the decorative arts of the period represented — 1903-1920 — and the era immediately preceding it, the individual photographs will be presented with some commentary on the objects present in the rooms, including their style, background, and probable origin.

Early Cabins

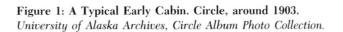

Certainly the rough miner's log cabin was prevalent in the early mining camps. The cabin shown in Figure 1 is in Circle, around 1903, and is an especially tidy version of the genre. However, as this photo illustrates, even the most modest dwellings had many manufactured goods and objects and usually an attempt was made to create a homelike atmosphere. For though this was indeed the frontier, just behind the prospectors were the merchants and purveyors of goods who would create the towns to follow.

In any case, many of the elements deemed necessary to create a homelike atmosphere in the first part of the century could be easily transported. Nel Lawing's cabin (Figure 4) illustrates not only how much could be

Figure 1: A Typical Early Cabin. Circle, around 1903.
University of Alaska Archives, Circle Album Photo Collection.

1

Figures 2 & 3: Cabin Interior. Circle, around 1903.
University of Alaska Archives, Circle Album Photo Collection.

This is probably the interior of the cabin in Figure 1.

accomplished with small, portable objects like pictures, fabric, and bric-a-brac, but also that the desire was to create a familiar, tasteful, artistic and homelike atmosphere even among those who had come so far from familiar cities and towns. Alaskan pioneers were not a group fleeing conventional aspirations, but rather a group who hoped, by participating in the goldrush, to gain more rapidly the accouterments of success.

Figure 4: Nel Lawing or Alaska Nellie's Cabin. Probably at Council, 1902-3.
"What Artistic taste and refinement can do in an Alaskan cabin."
University of Alaska Archives, Ben Mozee Collection.

Background History of Decorative Arts of the Period

It might be well to review at this point exactly what defined and constituted the good taste and artistic effect toward which Alaskan pioneers, as others of their era elsewhere, strived. Two trends predominate in the characteristic "look" of most of the collected photographs. The first can loosely be termed "Victorian" and includes some of the underlying characteristics of the jumble of Victorian styles. The second, which will here be called the Mission style, superceded the Victorian style starting around 1901. In spite of the fact that there was never one actual Victorian style, because the term and image are so pervasive, a review of Victorian taste is important to the understanding of what remained of it in the last decades of the 19th century, and what followed.

Victorian Style

In America, the Victorian era is generally recognized as the period between 1867 and 1901. Rather than being a distinct style, however, it was more a point of view envisioning the sanctity and desirability of home and family life. The Victorian period witnessed a parade of styles each of which was thought to more perfectly embody the expression of that point of view. Early Victorian styles followed their predecessors in being distinct period revivals or distinct furniture styles advocated for the furnishing of entire rooms. Thus Victorian Classical, popular from 1830-1850 and disdained thereafter, followed the Early Queen Anne, Chippendale, Federal, and Empire styles of the late 18th and early 19th centuries. The Gothic Revival was inspired by the rebuilding of the English houses of Parliament in 1836, and grew as it was popularized by Andrew Jackson Downing with his *Architecture of Country Houses* in 1850. Downing's cottages with their steep gables and gingerbread and fretwork detailing are still popularly recognized as Victorian. Elizabethan, Rococo, Italianate, and Renaissance styles all had their proponents in the period before 1870. Finally, the period between 1865 and 1895 became known as the Eclectic Decades, eclectic here meaning a little of everything. Eclectic came to include English, French, and Renaissance Revivals as well as the exotic styles, Moorish, Turkish, Oriental, Japanese, and even Egyptian and Aztec.

Amid this welter of emulation and adaptation should be noted the rise of the Aesthetic Movement, Charles Eastlake, William Morris and the English Arts and Crafts. William Morris, an artist, was the founder of the English Arts and Crafts movement, a movement away from the overdone and mass produced detailing of the revival styles. He advocated a return to honest craft and originality in one-of-a-kind decorative pieces of architectural ornament and furnishings. His fabrics and wallcoverings were hand block printed originals and many of his designs were taken from nature. The style of his Morris and Co. designs and furnishings caught on however, and were widely copied, adapted and reproduced both in England and America.

Building on similar foundations Charles Eastlake, an English architect, also advocated a return to honest furnishings. However, for his models he turned to medieval furniture, massive pieces often with Gothic styling and handcarved detail. Eastlake's publication *Hints On Household Taste* published in 1868, remained popular throughout five American printings between 1872 and 1881. The Aesthetic Movement in England was mirrored by one in America, advanced through the work of Louis Comfort Tiffany, later to be known for his more Art Nouveau glasswork, and other artists who put their talents to work in the decorative arts through the interior design firm of Louis C. Tiffany and Co., started in 1879.

Through this parade of style and philosophy that developed by the last decades of the 19th century, ran some common characteristics of interior decoration. By the time the styles were distilled in many how-to books and ladies magazines and produced in inexpensive versions for popular consumption, it was only the most basic characteristics that remained. These characteristics included the use of, and juxtaposition of many different patterns in the same room; elaborateness, that is superimposed decorations, such as valances, scarves, fringes, ribbons, etc., applied to individual objects and to the whole setting; and the use of manufactured decorative objects produced and advertised to enhance an artistic effect. Art-units, or the arrangement of objects on a mantle, shelf, or portion of the wall into a sort of still life for an artistic effect and the overall crowded total effect were also characteristic.

Thus, the overall impression of a Victorian parlour is a crowded welter of juxtaposed patterns and elaborated objects from various periods. By the last decades of the 19th century the Victorian style was inclusive, rather that exclusive. While the overall color scheme was supposed to be coordinated, patterns and objects from many of the various styles were often mixed. Morris style papers, Eastlake and Revival furniture, Turkish chairs and table covers, and Moorish portieres. "Artistic pieces" including sculpture, vases, statuettes,

Figure 5: A Characteristically Victorian Use of Pattern. Valdez, 1904.
University of Alaska Archives, Mary Whalen Collection.
Photographer: P. S. Hunt, Photo No. E39.

china and more were mixed with "Household Elegancies", ribbon and fabric adornments, needlework, and even rustic furniture and picture frames.[1]

Nearly universal to the period was wallpaper. By the 1880s certainly, all manner of manufactured wallpapers were available as well as all manner of advice on their use. The most popular scheme advocated a three part division of the wall into dado, the lower part of the wall sometimes paneled with wood wainscot, the wall or filling which was the main body of the wall, and the frieze, directly below the ceiling. Additional decorative borders between sections were also used. These schemes were common to all of the various styles.[2]

Some of the most popular Victorian themes remained popular even after the end of the Victorian era and were often then mixed with later pieces and styles. Most notable are the use of wallpaper, the persistent interest in things Japanese, the persistent use of portieres, often of exotic origin, and the mixing of styles themselves.

Also of note was the Victorian fascination with the Rustic or Western style. This is perhaps best illustrated by the example of the noted Philadelphia architect Frank Furness who brought back from his summers in the Rockies enough animal trophies to furnish a smoking room which was constructed of rough cedar and cedar saplings and nearly papered in engravings of the West.[3] The romantic West portrayed in magazines was the motivation for the development of a Rustic style, used in great Eastern summer homes and to a lesser extent, as an Indian motif for fabrics, furniture and wallcoverings.

This Rustic style should be born in mind when we see rustic pieces and especially fur rugs and throws in our Alaskan interiors, they may be more than just a necessity.

The Arts and Crafts Movement

Because the most common mental image of a gold rush town is of Victorian parlours, the single most surprising aspect of our Fairbanks photos was the repeated appearance of Arts and Crafts or Mission furniture. The first clue was the heavy oak settle-chair in the foreground of the photo of the Whitely family home in Fairbanks, Figure 6. This distinctive heavy oak chair with arms mortised into corner posts and at the same height and continuous with the chair back, is an unusual piece and definitely un-Victorian. It is represented in the catalog of L&JG Stickley, although it may not be an original. Chairs of this type were probably never common anywhere and certainly never as popularly pervasive as the round oak tables or Morris chairs of the same style. It characterizes the Mission style, an unusual, refined, and definitely un-Victorian taste. These simply designed, un-ornamented, dark, heavy pieces of furniture dominate sparsley furnished rooms and represent a tie between the Arts and Crafts movement of the beginning of the century and these small pioneer homes on the frontier.

Gustav Stickley and Craftsman Furniture

"I had no idea of attempting to create a new style, but merely to make furniture which would be simple, durable, comfortable, and fitted for the place it was to occupy and the work it had to do."

Thus said Gustav Stickley of his Craftsman furniture. Made of solid oak and crafted by workmen at his shops in upstate New York, the simple, solid looking furniture was meant to be symbolic of a philosophy that embraced craftsmanship, simple living, and socialistic concepts.

Stickley's furnishings and philosophy were an outgrowth of the earlier Arts and Crafts Societies in England at the latter part of the 19th century, brought to prominence by William Morris. The years 1893-1901 saw the first of dozens of Arts and Crafts Societies founded in the United States.

It was in 1901 that Gustav Stickley first exhibited his Craftsman furniture to general acclaim at the Pan-American Exposition in Buffalo, New York. The Arts and Crafts movement continued to grow in the period before the First World War. The movement encompassed craftspeople working in ceramics, glass and metal, as well as all of the decorative arts including furniture, textiles and wallpaper. The various societies held exhibits and sponsored lectures and classes throughout the Eastern seaboard and the Midwest as well as in the larger cities on the West Coast. Other furniture companies grew to prominence as well, including Elbert Hubbard and his Roycrofters, an artistic community in East Aurora, New York. The movement as a whole continued for some time to attach a moral righteousness to its style of simple design, natural materials, and refined ornament.

At his height, Stickley promoted the style through his own magazine, *The Craftsman*, and had his own building in New York City. The magazine

Figure 6: Craftsman Furniture on the Frontier. Fairbanks, 1912.
University of Alaska Archives, James Whiteley Collection.

Figure 7: "Furniture Dept. Upper Floor Valdez Bank and Mercantile Co., Inc."
University of Alaska Archives, Mary Whalen Collection.
Photographer: P. S. Hunt, Photo No. G2861.

promoted the benefits of country life, gave instructions for home crafts, and included home plans for Craftsman Houses with detailed illustrations. As the Craftsman house evolved into the popular and mass-produced bungalow, so Stickley's handcrafted furniture evolved into a popular style.

By 1909, Stickley was hounded by an army of imitators, including his brothers and their various firms and the so-called Mission style was included in the Sears catalog and probably in the lines of other popular furniture manufacturers as well.

Though the Mission style may have had its roots in the Craftsman furniture of upstate New York, a contemporary movement was ongoing in the Midwest — that of Frank Lloyd Wright and his contemporaries of the Prairie School. The Prairie School also emphasized simplicity of design, solidity, lack of ornamentation, and a return to basics. In fact Wright, George Maher, Grant Elmsie, and other practitioners of the Prairie School in Illinois, Wisconsin, Minnesota and Iowa, frequently designed furniture for their clients. Featured in such popular magazines as *Home and Gardens*, these architect designed pieces can also be considered as roots of the Mission style. In fact, the Sears catalog of 1908 in the promotional tag given to its Mission chairs, extols the style as the one being specified by many famous architects.

On the West Coast a contemporary Arts and Crafts style can be seen in the work of architects Greene and Greene, who specified Gustav Stickley's original Craftsman furniture for some of the upstairs rooms of the Gamble House for which they designed much of the furniture themselves.

The bungalows which were the popularized, mass-produced outgrowth of Craftsman and Prairie School houses were extremely popular on the West Coast, whose cities were rapidly expanding during this period. Many bungalows can still be seen in Seattle, whose rapid growth was in part fueled by its position as the gateway to Alaska. Mission or Craftsman style interiors spread in popularity along with the bungalows they were part of.

Furnishing the Pioneer Home

Unlike the immigrants to the American West, few of the men and women who came to Alaska were able to bring their household furnishings. Intending to strike it rich and then return home, they camped in tents on the beaches of Nome, rented a room in Valdez, and then moved on over the trail to Fairbanks or Ruby following rumors of the next big strike. People arrived with nothing but an "outfit," food to last the winter and the tools necessary to survive and dig for gold. The cabins and rooms they inhabited had a temporary and yet familiar look about them, much like young people today who arrive with nothing but a backpack and set up housekeeping in a cabin. These homes look like those of people we know. Finally, many did settle down, and the homes they established were furnished with things newly bought and thus in the latest style. Almost every object we see in these photos is contemporary with the period.

A variety of stores sprang up to serve this need like the Valdez Bank and Mercantile Co. pictured in Figure 7. Like the curious relationship between taste and merchandising today, the household taste of the residents of Valdez was undoubtedly shaped by what was available locally.

In the photo we see oriental rugs and Brussels carpeting prominently displayed. A rocking chair is exhibited along with a round and a square oak table and a stack of office chairs, among other items.

In addition, the services of painting and paperhanging were locally available. The Pioneer Wallpaper and Paint Store in Valdez advertised in the Valdez News "Paper-Hanging; Sign Writing; House Painting; Decorating."[4] Household furnishings could be ordered from stores in Seattle and shipped up, and of course the Sears, Wards and other catalogs had furniture as well as wallpaper, curtains, portieres, tablecloths, light fixtures and nearly everything else that could be needed to furnish a home. A perusal of the social column of any newspaper of the day will confirm that Alaskans were accustomed to travelling Outside and undoubtedly, just as we do now, they shopped for special items that were unavailable locally.

Figure 8: P. S. Hunt Self-Portrait. Valdez, April, 1911.
University of Alaska Archives, Mary Whalen Collection.
Photographer: P. S. Hunt, Photo No. G3578.

Methodology

Without the remarkable talent of photographer P. S. Hunt, this work would not have been possible. Hunt was a commercial photographer who moved north from San Francisco around 1898. His earliest photo of Valdez dates from 1902. He established himself there as a commercial photographer for the next 12 years, photographing many local scenes and a large number of portraits. He travelled quite a bit during those years photographing Cordova, Homer, Seward, the Aleutians, the trail to Fairbanks, the Copper River Valley and mining activities, Fort Liscomb and more; almost everything of interest.

P. S Hunt's interest in photographing interiors was unusual. Although photographers of American Interiors are not now considered as rare as they once were thought to be, still the over 100 photographs in this collection stands out as a monument.[5]

This remarkable series of portraits of homes in Valdez leads naturally to a curiosity about the homes, their owners and occupants, and about Hunt himself. We can surmise that Hunt photographed the homes of his friends and acquaintances as an artistic activity. The rooms look tidy, in most cases, cleaned up for the photographer. (See Figures 37, 38 & 39 for a "before" and "after" view.) Careful study of various series of two and three photographs of the same rooms reveals that Hunt occasionally moved furniture and objects, composing the room for his photographs. (As in Figures 34-36.) In one case, Figure 46, the roller shade over the window appears to be both up and down. Hunt apparently photographed it in both positions over a time exposure.

Many of the other photographs are of a documentary nature as well. Some were undoubtedly to convince those at home that Alaskans did not all live in igloos as with the photographs of the McGowan and Myers's Residences in Fairbanks, Figures 72, 73, & 74. These were published in a 1916 publication *Descriptive of Fairbanks* alongside the following commentary, "A very large percentage of the residents own their own homes, among these being many large frame buildings handsomely constructed and elegantly furnished, practically all of these being electrically lighted and many of them being steam heated." Of course, some of the photographs come to us as a by-product of photographing an event; a wedding, anniversary, or birthday party, (see Ellen Capwell's birthday party in Ruby, Figure 76), or a meeting of the Volunteer Fire Department in Council, (see Figure 79). Over 3,000 of P. S. Hunt's glass plate negatives are at the University of Alaska Archives at Fairbanks. Unfortunately, none of Hunt's own notes or records were saved and the plates were in a jumbled order when retrieved by the Archives. However, many of his plates were dated by him and these dates are noted in the Accession List. A dated order for Hunt's photographs was created thanks to the meticulous chronological numbering system which he used.[6]

1904 — 1907

The next seven photos comprise an extraordinary series of pictures of one house that is most unusual. Besides photos of the living and dining rooms, within the consecutive series of numbers are photos of a bathroom and bedroom. The date is presumed from P. S. Hunt's own numbering system to be around 1904 and the overall style of the interiors would seem to confirm this. It is thus one of the earliest homes in our series.

P. S. Hunt's artistry in composing and photographing these rooms, as well as the fact that he includes not only a bedroom but the only bathroom pictured in the entire collection, and that it is the first of his series of interiors, leads to the indelible suspicion that this is his own home in Valdez. Photos of his studio (Figure 58), testify to the same love of pattern that has created these rooms. But, though there is a resemblance, the man and woman glimpsed in these photos cannot be positively identified as Mr. and Mrs. Hunt.

Figure 9: Dining Area. Valdez, 1904.
University of Alaska Archives, Mary Whalen Collection.
Photographer: P. S. Hunt, Photo No. E30.

The juxtaposition of the ornate wallpaper pattern and the equally ornate woven, fringed cover on the table set the tone for the whole house. Through the doorway we can glimpse the living room portrayed in the next four photos. Studying this photo and Figure 11 we can surmise that this table is on one wall of the kitchen.

Overleaf

Figure 10: (Top Left) Cozy Corner. Valdez, 1904.
University of Alaska Archives, Mary Whalen Collection.
Photographer: P. S. Hunt, Photo No. E32.

This typical cozy corner consists of an Indian print throw cover on a daybed and extended up the wall accented with a variety of fancy pillows. The Victorian habit of juxtaposition of pattern and texture is very evident in these rooms and throughout this house. Here, the throw and the wallpaper and the portiere are all contrasting patterns. The view through the doorway is blocked by a curtained, folding screen. The door is trimmed with natural grained wood and the portiere hangs from a simple curtain rod.

Figure 11: (Top Right) Cozy Corner With View Into Kitchen Valdez, 1904.
University of Alaska Archives, Mary Whalen Collection.
Photographer: P. S. Hunt, Photo No. E40.

Another view of the same wall shows the kitchen through the open doorway, a woodstove, and a curtained closet with a cushioned, pressback rocking chair. The kitchen features a handpump over a shallow sink. The floor is covered with what might be a linoleum cloth which appears to run up the lower wall. Above is another wallpaper, again the whole emphasizing complexity and pattern. Here we can also see the carpet, a manufactured one with a large rather bold pattern. Note the bare electric lightbulb just at the top of the photo.

Figure 12: (Bottom Left) Living Room. Valdez, 1904.
University of Alaska Archives, Mary Whalen Collection.
Photographer: P. S. Hunt, Photo No. E38.

Continuing around the room we see a very Victorian composition of pattern and objects. There is a parlour table with a Turkish cover, another and different curtained folding screen, and another rocking chair in front of a window with a wonderful pair of lace curtains which hang nearly to the floor. A rather romantic style bust of a Greek hero sits on a second parlour table, this one with a lace cover. Notice the reflection in the ornately framed mirror of the woman seated in the cozy corner of the previous photos.

Figure 13: (Bottom Right) Living Room. Valdez, 1904.
University of Alaska Archives, Mary Whalen Collection.
Photographer: P. S. Hunt, Photo No. E33.

The folding screen, the two rocking chairs, and the parlour table with Turkish throw appear again here in another corner with a curtained set of shelves and the wallpaper background of Figures 10 and 11. There is an oval mirror with a white frame on the wall and there are a variety of personal photos displayed.

Figure 14: Bathroom. Valdez, 1904.
University of Alaska Archives, Mary Whalen Collection.
Photographer: P. S. Hunt, Photo No. E29.

The bathroom is the first photo numerically in the series. (It should be noted that the Whalen collection is not necessarily comprehensive and Hunt could have originally taken more photos in this series of a single house.)

The tile-look wallpaper together with the bathtub gives an overall modern look to the bathroom though it is quickly obvious that the tub is not plumbed. The facilities actually consist of the porcelain chamber pot and the china washbowl and pitcher on the washstand. Notice the mirror on the wall with the toothbrush and cup holder. There is a metal cafe chair and the floor is covered with a small oriental pattern rug.

Figure 15: Bedroom. Valdez, 1904.
University of Alaska Archives, Mary Whalen Collection.
Photographer: P. S. Hunt, Photo No. E31.

Figure 15, Hunt's photo E31, falls in the middle of the series we have just seen. Thus we can assume that it is in the same house. It appears to be an upstairs bedroom with a dormer window. The bedroom is furnished with a lovely brass and iron bed with a white coverlet and papered with what we might think of as a typical bedroom wallpaper. The Golden Oak, bowfront dressing table has an oval mirror with beveled glass. A small rocker with a cane seat shares the dormer window with a parlour table holding a selection of books. There is a small Persian rug on the floor and the fancy ruffled organdy sheer curtains are knotted at the side for a more artistic effect.

This is the corner of a kitchen with a view into the pantry. The walls of this kitchen are paneled with dark wood — horizontal above and vertical wainscoting below. The material on the floor is probably a patterned linoleum or oilcloth. There are two tables in the room, a work table covered with an oilcloth and a dining table with a heavy fringed tapestry cover as in the kitchen in Figure 9. Next to the dining table is a common pressback chair of the type available for a few dollars at the time. An electric light with a little ruffled glass shade hangs from the ceiling. The pantry is fixed up to be hidden by an ornate pair of portiere curtains which are tied up and out of the way giving us a rare glimpse of everday objects, photographed in such detail that one can almost identify the china patterns. Each shelf is covered with a bit of paper lace making a valance. On the top shelf are a variety of unmatched teacups hanging from cuphooks and stacked saucers beneath. Best plates of different patterns are displayed standing behind a variety of things on the second shelf, including a can of crab. A large jar of Horlick's malted milk dominates the packaged goods on the bottom shelf beneath which hangs a familiar enameled dishpan.

Figure 17: Kitchen. Valdez, March, 1905.
University of Alaska Archives, Mary Whalen Collection.
Photographer: P. S. Hunt, Photo No. G167.

The working end of the kitchen pictured here includes a kitchen cupboard made of a common car-siding or beaded board, a shallow sink with a handpump, a homemade worktable, and an ornate cookstove with a shiny copper water kettle. The floor is simple boards and the walls and sloping ceiling are papered with different papers. A bit of oilcloth is tacked up behind the sink. On a small shelf above the sink sits a mirror and a small clock, a dishtowel hangs below. Just to the left and almost out of the picture is a bow back kitchen chair. Curiously, framing the immediate foreground is what appears to be an iron and brass bedframe suggesting that this might be just a corner of a small cabin.

Note the use of fabric on the walls which was often used in log cabins instead of wallpaper. It was tacked up and then sized or painted with a sort of glue which made it shrink for a tight fit. Here, a dark material is used on the walls with a light patterned wallpaper for the ceiling. This room strives for a simple yet decorative effect with a variety of homemade furniture including the stool at the desk, the log plant stands and the end table with the lace scarf and flowers. The daybed was probably homemade as well and features a B.P.O.E. pillow. Sheer curtains are valanced rather than draped over the rod as we have seen in some of the photos from Valdez. Only the sewn together carpet, the small rug, the small rolltop desk, and the rocker are manufactured and storebought objects. Of interest are the rawhide wallhanging of an Indian and the small round wood picture frames displayed among other items above the daybed.

The interior of this cabin, although plain, has obviously been decorated. Note the double portiere with sheer material above and native blankets below to divide the living room and bedroom. The woman sits in a wicker rocker next to a dresser with a mirror of the type that might have been recently purchased from Sears. A smaller rocker is next to the iron-framed bed with a floral pattern cover. The little girl sits on an oriental pattern rug which is probably of domestic manufacture. In the corner of the living room is a Morris chair with striped upholstery. Note the display of an art vase, two carved wooden Indian heads, and a bust on the exposed rafters. Also note the white painted wainscoting with what appears to be a dark fabric wallcovering.

Figure 20: Miner in a Rented Room. Valdez, March, 1905.
University of Alaska Archives, Mary Whalen Collection.
Photographer: P. S. Hunt, Photo No. G168.

This neat room with its ornate wallpaper, iron and brass bed with chenille spread, and rocker with cushion is a long way from a miner's cabin. The wallpaper is of an ornate Victorian pattern which must have been up for some time by 1905. All of the furniture, including the pressback chairs, spindle leg table, the rocker, the kerosene lamp, and even the bed and the woodstove could have come from the local mercantile or the Sears catalog. Only the plat of some mining claims holding a prominent position on the wall and the photos and trivia on the table appear to belong to the miner. From the lone shelf hangs his Sunday best.

Figure 21: Reading. Valdez, January, 1906.
University of Alaska Archives, Mary Whalen Collection.
Photographer: P. S. Hunt, Photo No. G565.

A distinguished looking gentleman sits in a room furnished with a table with a batiked cover and embroidered pillow, a washstand with china bowl and pitcher, and a glass-front cabinet with only a few bottles and what could be dental or surgical instruments inside. A lace curtain is draped and tied over a curtain rod. Towels hang over the washstand. Note the mirror which is hung over a religious painting. The wallpaper is a stripe and flower bouquet pattern with a matching garland border above.

Figures 22 and 23: Pictures of a Baby. Valdez, August, 1905.
University of Alaska Archives, Mary Whalen Collection.
Photographer: P. S. Hunt, Photo Nos. G438 and G441.

These pictures of a baby have provided wonderful portraits of a parlour as well. Baby and dog play on an oriental style room-size rug laid over a painted wood floor. The door is stained dark while the woodwork is painted white. The sole piece of furniture is a reclining couch of a Victorian vintage with innumerable pillows which were quite fashionable, some of them have an almost Art Nouveau pattern. A single piece of lace hangs at the window from

the curtain rod to the floor. A little valance has been made out of the same material. The wallpaper is again a large Victorian pattern used all the way to the ceiling. Thus, although Victorian elements are used, the room has a more modern feeling with its all-over wallpaper and sparse furnishings and lack of knickknacks or art objects. Note the single bare bulb for electric lighting.

Figure 24: View of a Dining Room Through Doorway. Valdez, February, 1906.
University of Alaska Archives, Mary Whalen Collection.
Photographer: P. S. Hunt, Photo No. G628.

This view of a dining room and parlour illustrates many Victorian characteristics of room decor and arrangement. Two different types of wallpaper are used in the different rooms, both typical elaborate Victorian patterns. The wall scheme in the parlour includes a matching frieze with a small border between filling and freize. At the doorway an elaborate and very heavy portiere hangs from a brass rod. Two different carpets meet at the doorway as well. For this photo, a lyre back classic Revival chair is posed in the doorway. Note the portrait hanging across the corner with the small wooden spoons tied with ribbon below and the art picture above the doorway. All were rather late Victorian affectations. In the dining room, the sideboard also seems to be placed across the corner of the room, an arrangement we would not think of today. A great variety of cut glass is displayed on the sideboard and table.

The Tillicum Club

The Tillicum was a social club, hosting galas, card parties, receptions, and other social events. The building, as seen in Figure 25, was constructed much like a house and we can suppose that in furnishing it the goal was to be homelike. So it represents a kind of apothesis of taste of the period. It features a variety of comfortable and mostly new furniture. A very Victorian wallpaper pattern is used in all the rooms with a complimentary paper on the ceiling. Lace curtains with valances are used at the windows. The electric light fixtures with small bulbs and reflectors are rather unusual. Note the variety of native baskets displayed.

Figure 25: "Tillikum Club. Valdez, Alaska, May 6 '05."
University of Alaska Archives, Mary Whalen Collection.
Photographer: P. S. Hunt, Photo No. G223.

Figure 26: (Below)"Tillikum Club. Valdez, Alaska, May, 1905."
University of Alaska Archives, Mary Whalen Collection.
Photograher: P. S. Hunt, Photo No. G244.

Figure 27: (Opposite, Top) "Tillikum Club. Valdez, Alaska, 1905."
University of Alaska Archives, Mary Whalen Collection.
Photographer: P. S. Hunt, Photo No. G226.

Figure 28: (Opposite, Bottom) "Tillikum Club. Valdez, Alaska, 1905."
University of Alaska Archives, Mary Whalen Collection.
Photographer: P. S. Hunt, Photo No. G225.

Figure 29: Tillikum Club Card Party. Valdez, 1904.
University of Alaska Archives, Mary Whalen Collection.
Photographer: P. S. Hunt, Photo No. E27.

1908

The small calendar on the wall above the nightstand displays March, 1908. This date along with P. S. Hunt's number in the corner helps to date this and the following sequence of photos.

This is probably a man's rented room. Note the pipe on the bedside table, the boots against the wall and the spittoon, contrasting with the floral wallpaper, the bow tied to the back of the rocker, and the rather fancy dresser. An Indian blanket is used as a bedspread with satin pillows. A native basket and scenic photograph decorate the corner shelf. The plain wardrobe, possibly of local construction, holds a towel for the washstand and kerosene lamp while an electric light hangs from the ceiling. The night table with dresser scarf would have been called Queen Anne. Framed prints are augmented by photographs of a wife or sweetheart and local scenes.

Figure 30: Bed-Sitting Room. Valdez, March, 1908.
Anchorage Historical and Fine Arts Museum.
Photographer: P. S. Hunt, Photo No. G2824.

Figure 31: Two Rooms in a More Modern Style. Valdez, March, 1908.
University of Alaska Archives, Mary Whalen Collection. Photographer: P. S. Hunt, Photo No. G2816.

Oriental screen with view into back room.

Figure 32: Another View of the Same Room. Valdez, March, 1908.
University of Alaska Archives, Mary Whalen Collection. Photographer: P. S. Hunt, Photo No. G2810.

View from back room into front.

Two Rooms in a More Modern Style

These three photographs comprise a complete record of a home that was far more up-to-date than those we have seen so far. The body of the walls of both rooms are plain up to the frieze, which along with the ceiling is papered in a rather simple moire pattern. The desk, library table and record player stand are all Mission Oak pieces, probably of the mass-produced variety. On the desk is a Tiffany style lamp while the curtain hanging over the closet behind it also suggests the Art Nouveau. It is difficult to guess the use of the two rooms. From the arrangement of china displayed on the plate-rail in the front room and the two chairs pulled up to the desk, it appears that the room may have also been used for dining. Curtains in the back room are of plain cotton with drawn work and draped over a cafe rod. In the front room is a simple cotton ruffled curtain tied back on one side. The phonograph in the back room, as well as the guitar and mandolin on the day-bed, indicate the occupant's interest in music. The Japanese screen illustrates the popularity of things oriental in the Arts and Crafts period. The area hidden may have served as the dressing room with its mirror, a part of which can be glimpsed hanging on the wall. The dresser might have been called Golden Oak. The arrangement of personal objects suggests a bedroom but a study of all of the photos shows no bed except for the day-bed in the front room.

Figure 33: A Third View of the Same Room, View from Front Room into Back. Valdez, March, 1908.
University of Alaska Archives, Mary Whalen Collection.
Photographer: P. S. Hunt, Photo No. G2829.

Arranged for a Party

These three photos can be recognized as the same room by the unique fleur-de-lis wallpaper on the walls. In fact the furniture is the same in all three however, in Figures 35 and 36 it has been rearranged with new flowers added and presents displayed as if for a party. The use of furnishings suggests an easy co-existence of style and objects. Both the dining table and the occasional table are classic Mission Oak, as is the Morris chair. Note the exposed pegs on the occasional table and the simple lines of all the pieces. The wallpaper, carpet, and cozy corner were all holdovers from the earlier era. The massive black leather rocker was a perennial favorite and popular as a club chair, and who could resist a child's wicker rocker? Figure 35 shows the stairs which are carpeted and have no rail. The sideboard is a revival style. The portiere probably hides stairs to a basement. The kitchen can be glimpsed through a doorway. Just at the right side of the photo behind the curtain is a telephone. One of the gifts, visible in Figure 36, is an electric coffee percolator. Another is the spindle-legged occasional table.

Figure 34: Before the Party. Valdez, March, 1908.
University of Alaska Archives, Mary Whalen Collection.
Photographer: P. S. Hunt, Photo No. G2815.

Figure 35: Rearranged, With View Into the Kitchen. Valdez, March, 1908.
University of Alaska Archives,
Mary Whalen Collection.
Photographer: P. S. Hunt, Photo No. G2835.

Figure 36: Party Gifts. Valdez, March, 1908.
University of Alaska Archives,
Mary Whalen Collection.
Photographer: P. S. Hunt, Photo No. G2814.

Figure 37: All Cleaned Up.
Valdez, March, 1908.
University of Alaska Archives,
Mary Whalen Collection.
Photographer: P. S. Hunt,
Photo No. G2821.

Figure 38: Another View.
Valdez, March, 1908.
University of Alaska Archives,
Mary Whalen Collection.
Photographer: P. S. Hunt,
Photo No. G2823.

Attic Accomodations

These two gentlemen seem to be demonstrating just how comfortable attic accomodations can be, especially with such up-to-date convieniences as a Morris chair equipped with a book holder and a phonograph with records. They seem to share an interest in pin-ups as well, though the railroad man seems to favor western rodeo girls while the reader of books prefers ballet and dance. Otherwise the room consists of two daybeds with a profusion of collector pillows, but probably only one Morris chair, which has been moved from photo to photo. Notice its flowered chintz cushion protectors. The attic has only a board ceiling, painted white and decorated with a medallion quilt. Note the phonograph and records, the built-in dresser, native models, beadwork, and artifacts, photographs of local buildings and ships, the bearskin rug, and the Teddy bear.

Figure 39: Attic Accomodations. Valdez, March, 1908.
University of Alaska Archives, Mary Whalen Collection.
Photographer: P. S. Hunt, Photo No. G2822.

Figure 40: (Above) "Mrs. C. M. King's Apartment."
Valdez, March, 1908.
University of Alaska Archives,
Mary Whalen Collection.
Photographer: P. S. Hunt, Photo No. G2812.

Figure 41: (Left) Mrs. C. M. King.
Valdez, Probably in 1910.
University of Alaska Archives,
Mary Whalen Collection.
Photographer: P. S. Hunt, Photo No. G3430.

Figure 42: (Right) "Mrs. C. M. King's Apartment.
Valdez, Alaska." March, 1908.
University of Alaska Archives,
Mary Whalen Collection.
Photographer: P. S. Hunt, Photo No. G2832.

Mrs. C. M. King's Appartment

Mrs. King was a widow who owned the Red Cross Drug Store in Valdez until about 1910, after which she is no longer listed in the directories and her drugstore ceased to advertise as well. Her apartment, which perhaps was over the drugstore, would have been described as "artistic to a high degree." It is the arrangement of the objects here that attracts our attention. The large window is framed by a fretwork screen with a fringed valance below. Curtains are probably sheer, and apparently there were no shades beneath as Hunt usually pulled the shades in such photos to give a more even light. At this end of the room we can see a rustic three panel screen with a twig style frame and curtained with fabric. Also visible in Figure 40 is the four-bulb light fixture with three bare bulbs and one extension cord leading to a fourth bulb suspended over a mirror which can be seen in Figure 42.

Mrs. King's apartment was a simple room with a plain board floor and wood wainscoting also painted or stained and varnished a dark brown. The wallpaper is almost plain, with a very finely striped texture, and a small, whimsical border above the wainscot and below the elaborate Victorian pattern frieze. The ceiling is done in yet another pattern. A closet at the back of the room is curtained, with a fringed valance matching that of the front window. Bookcases at the right and a table behind the woodstove are also curtained. The major piece of furniture is a daybed covered with an Indian blanket with a crazy quilt and a variety of pillows. Over this couch is an overly large and heavily framed mirror. A small Eastlake washstand sits at the back of the room. The small iron table and two chairs also make an interesting addition to the room. Three bouquets of flowers enliven the space and along with the photographs, pictures, mementos, china, and personal objects displayed on almost every surface, give the room a most personal quality.

Figure 43: "Judge O. P. Hubbard's Residence. Valdez, Alaska," October, 1908.
University of Alaska Archives, Mary Whalen Collection.
Photographer: P. S. Hunt, Photo No. G2030.

That Figures 43 and 44 represent the same rooms is evident by matching the unique scenic wallpaper and the stencil lace curtains.

The dark painted wall together with the scenic frieze, the unusual curtains, and the prominently displayed collection of native baskets suggest at least a familiarity with some of the Arts and Crafts philosophy. However, the fringed valance, the Morris chair with spindles, carving, ornate legs and those menacing animal figureheads are decidedly out-of-date. O. P. Hubbard was at the least a lawyer and an owner or developer of some mining claims. However, I can find no mention of his having been a judge. His collection of law and other books is housed in the popular glass front bookcases which, by the way, do not match. The scenic wallpaper is worth remarking on. Scenic friezes were popular in both Medieval Revivals after Eastlake, and with the Arts and Crafts and Aesthetic styles, many of whose proponents were artists who would actually paint such works. Contrastingly, the English style in 19th century country houses always featured horse and dog paintings, including scenes from the hunt such as that pictured here. This marriage of the two styles reminds us of nothing so much as a 1930's Colonial Revival American living room and perhaps was a product of a Colonial Revival style which sprang up after the Philadelphia Centennial Exposition of 1876.

40

Figure 44: Another View of the Same House. Valdez, October, 1908.
University of Alaska Archives, Mary Whalen Collection.
Photographer: P. S. Hunt, Photo No. G2031.

This view shows the arrangement of the study and a dining room off of a wide central hall with a halltree holding a few hats. The overall feeling is of a more modern approach with the rather sparse furnishings and simple displays of objects. The two portieres on the double doorways are an Indian blanket and an apparently heavy, woven tapestry. The floors are covered with a variety of carpets leaving some of the wood floor exposed. Smaller rugs are used on top of the carpets.

Figure 45: Bedroom. Valdez, Fall, 1908.
University of Alaska Archives, Mary Whalen Collection.
Photographer: P. S. Hunt, Photo No. G2033.

This rather charming bedroom could, from the nearly consecutive numbering, be in the home of Judge O. P. Hubbard (Figures 43 and 44). The flowered wallpaper sets a light and airy tone picked up by the iron and brass bed with a white coverlet. White sheer counterpane curtains with a valance hang at the window. A French Golden Oak dresser with mirror and lace dresser scarf and a small secretary complete the furnishings. On the floor is a machine made carpet with a contrasting dark, bold pattern.

Figure 46: Kitchen. Valdez, March, 1908.
University of Alaska Archives, Mary Whalen Collection.
Photographer: P. S. Hunt, Photo No. G2825.

This tidy kitchen is very simply furnished. The small wood cookstove has a variety of utensils on it. The dry sink is really a piece of furniture with a cabinet underneath and a bucket for water. Two simple chairs are pulled up to the utilitarian wooden table with no cover. In the corner, a china cabinet displays the china. Notice the ironing board parked behind the cabinet. The wallpaper is of a tile pattern with a border and frieze and the floor is plain boards.

Figure 47: An Evening's Entertainment. Valdez, March, 1908.
University of Alaska Archives, Mary Whalen Collection.
Photographer: P. S. Hunt, Photo No. G2818.

The brash wallpaper with the matching frieze and a border between, sets the tone for this room. A different paper is used for the ceiling, while on the floor is a small Persian rug over Belgian carpeting of a geometric design. A Golden Oak fall-front desk serves as a stand for the phonograph with its painted speaker. Note the sheer curtains with an embroidery work border draped over a brass rod and with a roller shade behind. Displayed on the wall are a large, gilt-framed portrait, a few small matted photographs, a small piece of smoked moosehide, and a photo-portrait in a heavy oak frame. More photos are stored and displayed in the small native basket on the floor and on top of the curtained shelf unit which hangs just a little too close to the daybed. The man on the floor reads the *Valdez Daily Prospector*.

Figure 48: Living and Dining Room With View of Kitchen. Valdez, November, 1908.
University of Alaska Archives, Mary Whalen Collection.
Photographer: P. S. Hunt, Photo No. G2060.

Another eclectic set of rooms where arrangements and objects of different styles co-exist. The living room shows a mix of a plain, dark, painted wall with a very ornate wallpaper frieze. Another paper is used on the ceiling and a third on the walls of the dining room beyond. A sateen valance with fringe decorates the doorway. Featured are a piano and a woodstove with an ornately embroidered cushion displayed prominently on a rather plain chair. On the opposite wall are some homemade shelves that have been covered with fabric and hold a variety of objects of everyday use, plus a few native baskets. A very plain carpet is used in the dining room despite the very showy wallpaper. A curved glass china cabinet of the manufactured Golden Oak style popular around 1902 holds a collection of crystal or cut glass and displays a chafing dish and a kettle with burner. The claw-footed round dining table is covered with an embroidered table cloth.

Figure 49: Chauncey Cowden Residence. Nome, 1908.
Anchorage Historical and Fine Arts Museum. Collection No.: B65. 18. 242.

This unusual room displays a variety of styles. The striped wallpaper is topped with a wood picture rail and a restrained paper on the frieze and ceiling. Note the gas fixture at the ceiling with gas line leading to a companion table fixture. The shelf on the far wall is decorated in the manner of an art unit with a tapestry valance. The curving lines of the glass door bookcase indicates an Art Nouveau influence. The owner displays a large collection of photos, pictures and objects of wide variety. Note the Japanese print, busts and statuettes, and elaborate vases. An oriental carpet covers most of the painted wooden floor.

1909 — 1911

Figure 50: Corner of a Bedroom. Valdez, February, 1909.
University of Alaska Archives, Mary Whalen Collection.
Photographer: P. S. Hunt, Photo No. G2807.

The calendar on the wall and the New Year's greeting on the mirror both indicate a date of February, 1909 for this photo which is probably the corner of a bedroom. The dresser mirror and the wall display a collection of photo portraits. The matching washstand has toweling on top and holds the washbasin and pitcher as well as a smaller pitcher, a cup with toothbrush, a bottle of mouthwash or patent medicine, and a German beer stein. The wallpaper is an ornate Victorian pattern and at the window hangs a sheer lace curtain draped over the rod.

24th ANIVERSAY MR & MRS. P. S. HUNT.
VALDEZ. ALASKA. MAR. 29~09.

Figure 51: "24th Anniversary Mr. & Mrs. P. S. Hunt, Valdez, Alaska, Mar. 29- 09."
University of Alaska Archives, Mary Whalen Collection.
Photographer: P. S. Hunt, Photo No. G3553.

This photo of the anniversary dinner for Mr. & Mrs. Hunt shows a large group of people crowded into a small dining room. Note the dangerously meandering stovepipe, the table service, the mirror on the wall, the bare bulb, and the table turned partially on the diagonal to accommodate everyone. Mr. and Mrs. Hunt are seated in the center of the picture. One of their sons leans into the photo at the right.

Figure 52: Living Room/Bedroom with Phonograph. Valdez, May, 1909.
University of Alaska Archives, Mary Whalen Collection.
Photographer: P. S. Hunt, Photo No. G2210.

This is possibly the inside of a small, two room house or cabin used as both living room and bedroom. The second room in the house, behind the doorway in Figure 53, was probably a kitchen. This is again a very unusual Morris or Arts and Crafts inspired wallpaper with a pattern of leafy trees. Note the border between ceiling and wall of a matching scene with trees. The ceiling is covered with a light cloud pattern contrasting with the overall dark effect of the walls. Note the way the top of the stove pipe has been painted white so that it blends in with this distinction between wall and ceiling. A dark varnished wainscot completes the walls and the door and door trim are stained dark to complete the scheme. The plain board floor is left exposed here with only two small rugs. There are a variety of chairs of all types including a good Mission rocker and a rather ornate Morris chair. Note the telephone on the wall with a phone book tacked up next to it.

Figure 53: Living Room/Bedroom with Phonograph. Valdez, May, 1909.
University of Alaska Archives, Mary Whalen Collection.
Photographer: P. S. Hunt, Photo No. G2211.

The bed seems to have a burlap or hopsacking cover and is spruced up with pillows. The phonograph with the painted speaker horn plays cylinder records of which there is a good collection. Visible in this photo is an oak veneer rocker. A bare lightbulb hangs from the ceiling and a corner shelf holds a few knickknacks. Three small bags are displayed tacked to the wall. The portiere is closer to just a piece of fabric hung on a curtain rod in front of the door.

Figure 54: The Wedding Party. Valdez, November, 1909.
University of Alaska Archives, Mary Whalen Collection.
Photographer: P. S. Hunt, Photo No. G2545.

These two photos give us an interesting look at not only a room but a collection of everyday objects that were considered special enough to give as wedding gifts. The portrait of the wedding couple helps us to understand who the gifts were intended for, in this case, the couple appears older than the usual newlyweds — presumably they already had many household necessities. First, note the popularity of the parlour or occasional table itself; there are six in this photo — the one on the extreme right has a gift tag on it. China and crystal were popular gifts including hand-painted Bavarian china, candy dishes of various designs, a fine tea set on top of the piano, a variety of cut glass, and more than one cream and sugar set. There is a set of cutlery with bone handles, a chafing dish, a potted geranium, a thermos or flask, a framed picture (perhaps of a moose), two decorative busts, a copper tea kettle, perhaps a comforter tied up in what looks like a pillow case, and a variety of linens. The big gift was the veneer rocker and matching stool. On the rocker is an Arts and Crafts woven pillow with a cattail design. Also notice the lamp with a fringed glass shade on the table to the left.

The room itself is papered with border and matching frieze. The lace curtains have been draped over the rod and tied with an oversized knot for an artistic effect. The room has been decorated with spruce boughs and colored lights, probably for the Christmas season.

G2546.

Figure 55: The Wedding Gifts. Valdez, November, 1909.
University of Alaska Archives, Mary Whalen Collection.
Photographer: P. S. Hunt, Photo No. G2546.

Figure 56: "Fred Cowden at Home. Nome, Alaska." Before 1910.
Anchorage Historical and Fine Arts Museum, Collection No.: B6. 5. 18. 80.

The light in this picture creates an artistic effect and though we cannot
see much of the room, the overall impression is decidedly un-Victorian. The
profusion of plants must have been quite a rarity in Nome. This photo and
the following one have the same unusual paneling, a plain wall with wood
lathe trim. In this photo, small photographs or pictures are arranged vertically
on the panels. Beneath is a daybed with the typical profusion of large pillows.
The woodstove is an especially ornate one — it should be remembered that
when Nome was founded in 1900, the Victorian era was still in full swing.
By 1910 it had shrunk considerably. In fact, Fred Cowden himself left around
1910. When towns are new or expanding, much furniture is brought in new,
but when they are contracting, people collect what is already there from those
who are leaving. And so the ornate stove, the older style Morris chair, and
the square pedestal table as well as much of the furniture in the following
photo are probably older.

Figure 57: Another View of Fred Cowden's Home. Nome, Alaska, Before 1910.
Anchorage Historical and Fine Arts Museum, Collection No.: B6. 5. 18. 76.

Though the furnishings are of an older style, the overall impression is of the Arts and Crafts era with the plain paneled walls, a very simple portiere, the art-pottery plate of Japanese design on the plate rail, and the lack of conflicting or contrasting patterns or fussy art units.

Figure 58: P. S. Hunt's Studio. Valdez, June, 1911.
University of Alaska Archives, Mary Whalen Collection.
Photographer: P. S. Hunt Photo No. G3624.

    P. S. Hunt's studio in 1911 was a rather utilitarian space with wallpaper that by this time was quite out-of-date. He displays a mix of patterns on walls, portieres, ceiling, and curtained storage that is more typically Victorian. It presents quite a contrast with the office in the next photo.

75-84-1997

Figure 59: Anonymous Office. Valdez, December, 1911.
University of Alaska Archives, Mary Whalen Collection.
Photographer: P. S. Hunt Photo (no number).

Is this man a newspaperman or a stock broker? It looks like he is thumbing through a pile of bonds or property deeds. The office appears to have a plain dark wallpaper to a picture rail height, topped with a minute border and a poorly applied wallpaper frieze. The simple, draped lace curtain is backed by a dark shade. The "horse" calender on the wall shows December, 1911 and an issue of the *Valdez Daily Prospector* is displayed prominently on the daybed which holds stacks of papers and magazines. The office equipment includes a rolltop desk with bookcase above, swivel oak chair, Remington typewriter, and telephone with phonebook. It is lit with a bare bulb contrived to hang over the desk. Rock samples sit under the typewriter table and a Dall sheep trophy head and stuffed bird complete the picture.

1912 — 1919

Figure 60: An Arts and Crafts Home. Valdez, April, 1912.
University of Alaska Archives, Mary Whalen Collection.
Photographer: P. S. Hunt, Photo No. G3804.

A very plain, very tasteful Arts and Crafts style pair of rooms with plain plastered walls and ceiling, plain dark wood trim, sheer curtains, and much Craftsman furniture, including the classic library table arranged on the diagonal in the center of the room, two Mission rockers, and the very squared-off wicker and leather rocker, a very small, plain secretary, and a small stool used as a plant stand. The ceramic pot on the stand would have been considered very modern art pottery. The Art Nouveau lamp on the library table was another very up-to-date piece. Note the use of native baskets, considered as indigenous Arts and Crafts. The floor is polished wood with a very plain carpet in the living room and an oriental style in the dining room. The plate rail in the dining room displays a variety of china. The sideboard and the dining table are older pieces as are the side chairs. The light fixtures however, with three small glass shades hanging on chain from a base at the ceiling are more modern and accentuate the Arts and Crafts look.

58

Figure 61: Another Arts and Crafts Home. Valdez, July, 1912.
University of Alaska Archives, Mary Whalen Collection.
Photographer: P. S. Hunt, Photo No. G3863.

This room features Craftsman style dark paneling to a picture rail displaying photographs and an art pottery vase. The walls and ceiling are entirely plain as is the sewn together carpet. A very nice Mission arm chair and footstool and a small Mission library table (again in the center of the room), are combined with two matching oak chairs of a less doctrinaire style, with leather upholstery and some spindle work on the legs. The library table is draped with an ornate shawl and holds a Tiffany style lamp. Notice that its cord goes to one of the sockets in the light fixture above, a common arrangement. In the corner is a small Mission Oak secretary displaying an older clock and another art pottery vase. Also notice the Arts and Crafts plant stand in front of the window. The corner of a much older piano with stool can be seen to the right. The curtains (frilly lace on curtain rods) provide a distinct contrast.

Figure 62: Titled "Home of Mr. and Mrs. Godski." Fairbanks, 1912-1916.
Seattle Historical Society, Alaska Bureau: Central I p. 64. Collection No.: 17779

Though this photograph is neatly titled "Home of Mr. and Mrs. Godski" in a photo album in the collection of the Seattle Historical Society, the room pictured is actually the same room as in the following photo, Figure 63, which is titled "Home of Frank Clark." The first clue is that the wall treatment is the same — dark walls topped by light moire paper and ceiling. On further examination, the unusual Queen Anne library table appears in both photos, as does the Mission Oak rocker. Detailed examination of the Tiffany style lamp and of the border pattern of the oriental carpet is conclusive. Even the border on the sheer curtains is the same. One of the photos is therefore mis-identified.

The photos depict the living and dining room area comprising the downstairs of a two-story house. A kitchen is probably beyond the door at the rear. An overall Arts and Crafts look is created with the wall treatment and simple furnishings which include a Mission Oak rocker in the foreground, a simple round oak table with a more ornate base, and a Mission Oak armchair at the library table. At the rear of the room is a daybed or couch with a fringed throw and abundant pillows. Shelves are built-in under the stairs. The plain board floor, which appears to be rough sawn spruce, is covered with three different oriental pattern rugs. Over the table is a very fine Tiffany lampshade. The sideboard is quite restrained, though not really a Mission style piece. The photographs in the elongated frames displayed over the sideboard were a popular part of the Mission style. B.P.O.E. memorabilia is displayed on the wall over the couch. Also notice the geraniums and the bear rug.

Figure 63: Titled "Home of Frank Clark." Fairbanks, 1912-1916.
Seattle Historical Society, Alaska Bureau: Central I p. 64. Collection No.: 17780.

Frank Clark was a pharmacist and by 1915 the proprietor of the Red Cross Drug Store in Fairbanks. Sometime between 1911 and 1915 he moved to a home at the corner of Cushman St. and 7th Avenue which this could be a photo of. The home pictured here is plain, in the Arts and Crafts Style, which is emphasized by the stair rail of simple construction with a square newell post and small square spindles. The piano in the corner is unusually restrained, with unfinished wood in place of the black finish and gold work on earlier models. The piano bench is a good example of Mission Oak as is the small plant stand at the foot of the stairs.

Figure 64: Whitley Family Residence. Fairbanks, 1912-1916.
University of Alaska Archives, James M. Whitely Collection, No. 74-95-22.

Figure 65: Whitley Family Residence. Fairbanks, 1912-1916.
University of Alaska Archives, James M. Whitely Collection, No. 74-95-23.

These two photos present a few fine Mission Oak pieces pictured in the Whitley family home in Fairbanks. In Figure 64 is a Mission Oak parlour table, a Morris Chair, and a rare Arts and Crafts lamp with a square base and geometric shade. Notice the square supports on the arms of the Morris chair in contrast to the more ornate ones in earlier photos. Figure 65 pictures a small Mission Oak secretary of very simple construction. There were many publications at the time with instructions on how to construct Mission Oak furniture at home. This could perhaps be an example of that trend.

Figure 66: "An Alaskan Home." Fairbanks, 1912-1916.
University of Alaska Archives, Margaret Lentz Collection, No.: 76-92-87.
Photographer: Wolfe, Photo No. 236.

This living room and bedroom features dark wallcovering with a flowered frieze above a small border and a different wallpaper on the ceiling. A leather upholstered Morris Chair is in the living room next to a tall chest of drawers. A symmetrical little display on the dresser, harkening back to the art units of the Victorian era, features an Art Nouveau style clock. The floorcovering, which could be an early example of patterned linoleum, is used with smaller oriental rugs on top. In this case the light fixture is a kerosene lamp with a fabric flounce for a shade. A small candle lamp sits on the small brass or ormolu table in the center of the room.

The bedroom, separated from the front room by curtains, is furnished with an iron bedframe, washstand, rocker, and sidechair. Note the stencil work on the window curtains which is matched by the pillow on the rocker, the curtains behind the wash stand, and the bedlinens. Home stenciling was an art encouraged by the Arts and Crafts movement and in fact described in how-to articles in Gustav Stickley's magazine *The Craftsman*.

Figure 67 (page 65); Figure 68 (left); Figure 69: (below); Leopold David Home. Knik, 1910-1916.
Anchorage Historical and Fine Arts Museum.

Leopold David was a pharmacist when he moved to Knik in 1910. He later studied law and was appointed a U. S. Commissioner in Knik before moving to Anchorage where he built a large and very up-to-date bungalow around 1917.[7] Figures 68 and 69 present two views of a single room in the David home in Knik. Here an unusual wallpaper in the Arts and Crafts style with border and matching frieze is used with a single panel lace curtain. A simple homemade bookcase holds Mr. David's extensive collection of books. The piano is draped with a fur rug. Figure 69 shows a Mission Oak rocker and a small glass front bookcase displaying a silver service and glassware as well as books, and a small guitar next to the piano. Figure 67 shows the same family piano as that in the previous photos but in a different room, pictured here at Christmas time. The walls are bare plaster and the ceiling is boards. The same fur throw covers the piano, but there is a different carpet and a different occasional table, this one in a faintly Queen Anne style with a very small Christmas tree surrounded by toys, dolls, a Teddy bear, and wrapped presents on the shelf underneath.

Figure70: Mrs. Kellum's House Decorated for a Reception. Fairbanks, After 1912.
Seattle Historical Society, Alaska Bureau: Central I p. 66, Collection No.: 17781.

Mr. Kellum, a lawyer, died between 1911-1915. Mrs. Kellum's house at 318 First Avenue, was a rather fancy one with elaborate, dark stained and varnished wood trim, a floral carpet, and steam heat (notice the elaborate radiator). The wallpaper is so restrained as to be almost of an Art Nouveau mood. The house is shown here decorated with garlands of flowers and greenery as well as flower arrangements on the table. An oil or watercolor seascape in a very plain wood frame hangs on the wall. The rather interesting table is in a Renaissance Revival style.

Figure 71: Home of R.G. Southworth. Fairbanks, After 1912.
Seattle Historical Society, Alaska Bureau: Central I p. 68, Collection No.: 17782.

Note the wall treatment similar to Figure 62, a dark wall to the picture rail with light wall and ceiling above, this time with a tiny Arts and Crafts style border between, and white painted door trim and baseboard in the dining room, with dark trim in the living room. The spare style and plain walls are a good expression of the overall Mission style, though in the dining room the composition is completed with a non-descript round oak table and two Queen Anne chairs. The fine Tiffany lamp represents the Art Nouveau while the unusual rope portiere was a Victorian feature. Another tapestry portiere hung on rings serves as a bedroom door. Just hidden behind the lamp and dining table is a wonderful and unusual Craftsman chair, far more original than the usual manufactured Mission Oak. The very light oak rocker in the living room is also rather unusual. The settings are completed with very fine carpets which could actually be orientals. R. G Southworth was at first a reporter and later the publisher of the *Fairbanks Times*. The house to which he moved after 1911 was at the N. E. corner of Wickersham and 4th Avenue.

Figure 72: Living Room, Residence of Judge McGowan. Fairbanks, 1915-1916.
Seattle Historical Society, Alaska Bureau: Central I p. 56, Collection No.: 17777.

One of this original series of three photographs of the interior of Judge McGowan's house was published in the 1916 brochure *Descriptive of Fairbanks*. It is also included in Mayhew and Myers *Documentary History of American Interiors* (pg. 319, Fig. 194). They describe it as "showing a mixture of Mission and Art Nouveau with the earlier Moorish style." The Turkish cozy corner had a daybed covered with an Indian print, flowered fabric used on the wall surrounded with molding, and a profusion of very oriental looking pillows. The walls featured white painted trim including a molding separating the darker lower wall from the lighter upper wall. The board ceiling is supported with log beams decorated with growing trained ivy.

Figure 73: Living Room, Residence of Judge McGowan. Fairbanks, 1915-1916.
Seattle Historical Society, Alaska Bureau: Central I p. 56 Collection No.: 17776.

The light fixture has a plain fluted shade, the table is a not too ornate round oak, and carpets are small imitation orientals on the bare wood floor. The Morris chair is a very elaborate one. Mayhew and Myers note, "Elongated pictures were typical of the Mission style, as were the steins," (displayed on bracketed shelves over the doorways). The doorways to the greenhouse in Figure 72 and the alcove in Figure 73 are themselves of interest. Wide wood trimmed openings with columns were a feature of the Craftsman cottage or bungalow style, yet are here used with unpeeled log columns, possibly for the artistic effect.

Figure 74: "Dr. R. R. Meyers's Residence. Fairbanks, Alaska; Decorated with natural flowers for reception. 1916."
Seattle Historical Society, Alaska Bureau: Central I p. 60, Collection No.: 17778.

Another living and dining room of generous proportions, the residence of Dr. Myers was of the same genre as the McGowan Residence, Figures 72 and 73. A fretwork frieze, popular with the earlier Queen Anne and Shingle style homes, spatially divides the room in two. A sewn floral carpet covers the floor, accented with two fur rugs and a small oriental one. The wallpaper at the frieze is a very flat floral design, different from a Victorian or Morris paper, and more reminiscent of the stylized Art Nouveau though it is used with a rather Victorian border topping a plain dark lower wall. There is quite a display of china on three shelves above a small table and on another shelf and plate rail behind the round oak dining table. Other furniture consists of a massive style leather platform rocker, two veneer oak side chairs, two different Mission Oak rockers and a piano. In the bedroom, divided from the living room by a portiere, is an ornate iron and brass bed with an Art Nouveau lamp hanging above it. There is a dresser with an oval mirror, a curtained closet opening, and an interesting series of artistic photographs on the wall over the bed. Everything in the room, including the fringed light fixture, is garlanded with flowers.

Figure 75: "Wedding Reception. Ruby, Alaska."
"Clemons Photo, Ruby, Alaska, 1913."
University of Alaska, Lulu Fairbanks Album.

Though the photograph of a wedding reception captures a home interior of 1913, Ruby, a mining supply center established on the Upper Yukon after 1911, was in style quite a bit behind Valdez, a Southcentral port, and even Fairbanks which was quite a bit larger and had been established for some time. Ruby apparently did not have electricity, as the light fixture is a two burner oil lamp. The Thonet or bentwood chairs were originally an Austrian invention. The table is well set with crystal and china.

Figure 76: "Miss Ellen Capewell's Sixth Birthday Party. Sept. 6, 1916; Ruby, Alaska."
University of Alaska, Lulu Fairbanks Album.
Photographer: Basil Clemons.

Ellen Capewell's birthday party was celebrated at a large table set up in what was probably the living room of her home; a generous sized room in a wood framed house with tall ceilings, a painted wood floor, and a large wood stove with a meandering fluepipe. The children are seated on a variety of bentback kitchen chairs plus a church pew. The wallpaper uses a very modern Arts and Crafts motif.

**Figure 77: "Essinoye Dining Room - Residence of Fred G. Noyes. Fairbanks, Alaska."
Around 1916.**
University of Alaska Archives, Charles Bunnell Collection.
Photographer: "Photo by Johnson".

   This very formal dining room was in the large house at Minnie and Illinois streets which is now the funeral home. The ornate mahogany furnishings and paneling are more typical of a Renaissance Revival which was going on concurrently with the Arts and Crafts movement and popular among a certain class of the newly wealthy and those who wished to imitate them and could afford to have their homes decorated. As can be seen, the table and eight chairs, the sideboard and the china cabinet are all of the same style and manufacture and in the massive mode. In fact, the whole room including the paneling and the coffered ceiling is designed as a complete whole. This contrasts with all of the previous homes where ingenuity and originality put together sometimes disparate objects to create a personal style.

Figure 78: "Arthur Williams Residence. Fairbanks, Alaska, 1919."
University of Alaska Archives, Charles Bunnell Collection.

This is the living room in the home now known as the Mary Lee Davis House at 410 Cowles Street. Mrs. Davis, an author, reported that she purchased it in 1923 and went on to add an open fireplace with open oak bookshelves on either side.

The house was constructed by Mr. Williams for his wife who was from San Francisco and refused to move to Fairbanks until she could be provided with all the comforts of home. The interior in this photo features an Art Nouveau wallpaper with border, a desk in the massive or Jacobean mode, a rope portiere, bear rug, an Art Nouveau light fixture, and two overstuffed armchairs in the English style. It also features an oak floor, rumored to be the first in Fairbanks.

Notes

1. This is described by Gwendolyn Wright in *Building the Dream, A Social History of Housing in America*, (Cambridge, Mass. 1981:) pp.107. Wright also quotes from Harriet Spofford: "Provided there is space to move about, without knocking over the furniture, there is hardly likely to be too much in the room." p.111.

2. Edgar deN. Mayhew and Minor Myers, Jr.; *A Documentary History of American Interiors*, (New York, 1980:) p.207.

3. See Mayhew and Myers, Figure 171, page 296.

4. *Valdez News*; March 14, 1903.

5. William Seale, *The Tasteful Interlude*, (New York, 1975,) "interior photographs are so rare for most of this period that a collection of several hundred - most of them documented - is in itself a curiosity." (p.10). But Mayhew and Myers say in 1980, "Illustrations are difficult to find for the early periods, but after the mid-nineteenth century hundreds of pictures can be found for each style." (p.xi-xii.) They have collected over 1500 photographs which are now at the Lyman Allen Museum in New London, Connecticut.

6. Nearly 500 of the dated photographs were entered into the Lotus program on an IBM-PC computer along with Hunt's number and the accession number. The computer sorted for a consecutive list according to Hunt's numbering system, which indeed produced a chronological list, enabling many of his numbered photographs to be dated to the month and year. A curious departure from this chronology occurred between numbers G2772 - July 4, 1910 and G3463 - Sept. 17, 1910. In between are photographs with dates between Sept., 1907 and February, 1908. Fifteen of the photographs of interiors are in this series. Fortunately, one of these, Figure 30, No. G2824, includes a calendar allowing us to date it to March, 1908. Possibly, Hunt photographed this series of rooms in 1908 but was unable to print them until later.

7. Michael E. Carberry, *Patterns of the Past*, (Anchorage, 1979,) p. 14.

Bibliography

Interiors

Mayhew, Edgar deN. and Minor Myers, Jr. *A Documentary History of American Interiors: From the Colonial Era to 1915*. New York: Charles Scribner's Sons, 1980.

Seale, William. *Recreating the Historic House Interior*. Nashville: American Association for State and Local History, 1979.

Seale, William. *The Tasteful Interlude; American Interiors Through the Camera's Eye, 1860-1917*. New York: Praeger Publishers, 1975.

The Arts and Crafts Movement

Clark, Robert Judson, Editor. *The Arts and Crafts Movement in America 1876-1916*. Princeton: Princeton University Press, 1972.

Sanders, Barry, Editor. *The Craftsman; An Anthology*. Santa Barbara: Peregrine Smith, Inc., 1978.

Stickley, Gustav. *Craftsman Furniture made by Gustav Stickley at The Craftsman Workshops, Eastwood, N.Y.* Copyright 1909. Watkins Glen: The American Life Foundation, 1978.

Stickley, Gustav. *More Craftsman Homes; Floor Plans and Illustrations for 78 Mission Style Dwellings*. New York: Craftsman Publishing, 1912. Reprint. New York: Dover Publications, Inc., 1982.

Stickley, L. & J.G. *The Arts and Crafts Furniture Work of L. & J.G. Stickley*. Watkins Glen: The American Life Foundation, 1978.

Reference

Amory, Cleveland. *The 1902 Edition of the Sears Roebuck Catalogue*. New York: Crown Publishers, 1969.

Bridgeman, Harriet and Elizabeth Drury, Editors. *The Encyclopedia of Victoriana*. New York: Macmillan, 1975.

Nylander, Jane C. *Fabrics for Historic Buildings*. Washington: The Preservation Press, 1983.

Nylander, Richard C. *Wallpapers for Historic Buildings*. Washington: The Preservation Press, 1983.

Background

Brooks, H. Allen. *The Prairie School, Frank Lloyd Wright and his Midwest Contemporaries*. New York: W.W. Norton, 1976.

Fitch, James Marston. *American Building: The Historical Forces that Shaped It*. Second Edition. New York: Schoken Books, 1966.

Scully, Vincent J., Jr. *The Shingle Style and the Stick Style*. New Haven: Yale University Press, 1974.

Wright, Gwendolyn. *Building the Dream; The Social History of Housing in America*. Cambridge: MIT Press, 1981.

Guides to the Styles

Whiffen, Marcus. *American Architecture Since 1780: A Guide to the Styles*. Cambridge, Mass.: MIT Press, 1969.

McAlester, Virginia and Lee. *A Field Guide to American Houses*. New York: Alfred A. Knopf, 1984.

Rifkind, Carole. *A Field Guide to American Architecture*. New York: New American Library, 1980.

Dictionaries

Pierce, James Smith. *From Abacus to Zeus*. Englewood Cliffs, New Jersey: Prentice-Hall, 1968.

Saylor, Henry H. *Dictionary of Architecture*. New York: John Wiley and Sons, 1952.

Fleming, John; Fleming, Honour; Fleming, Hugh; and Pevsner, Nikolaus. *The Penguin Dictionary of Architecture*. New York: Penguin Books, 1966, 1979.

Harris, Cyril M. *Illustrated Dictionary of Historic Architecture*. New York: Dover Publications, 1977.

Alaska Homes

Carberry, Michael E. *Patterns of the Past: An Inventory of Anchorage's Heritage Resources*. Municipality of Anchorage, 1979.

Hart, Betsy. *The History of Ruby, Alaska, "The Gem of the Yukon"*. Anchorage: Village History Project, U.S. Dept. of the Interior, 1981.

Matheson, Janet. *Fairbanks; A City Historic Buildings Survey*. City of Fairbanks, 1978.

Index

"Trustees, Council City V. F. D."

83